AGUAS/WATERS

AGUAS/WATERS

Selected Poems of
Miguel Avero

Translated by
Jona Colson

Washington Writers' Publishing House
Washington, DC

Praise for *Aguas/Waters*

Uruguay is a country full of poetry, more and more available in bilingual editions in the U.S. Now we are lucky to have the wonderful *Aguas/Waters* by Miguel Avero in a translation by Jona Colson that moves Avero's Spanish into fluid and musical English. Avero is a poet of identity, history, and memory and *Aguas/Waters* is a book that sings, that carries you from the first poem to the last, each alert to the terrible beauty of life.

–Jesse Lee Kercheval, Editor of *América Invertida:*
An Anthology of Emerging Uruguayan Poets

Aquí dos libros de Miguel Avero para que el lector angloparlante pueda sumergirse en su poesía. Su inicial, consistente y límpido: *Arca de Aserrín*. Su doméstico, intertextual y profundo: *La Pieza*. Un autor, joven en edad y maduro en su escritura, con 7 libros en su haber, que tengo la fortuna de conocer personalmente y leer nuevamente, en esta hidratante selección de Jona Colson. Aquí su obra es un ventanal abierto al ayer que transforma a los lectores en niños mirando el cielo y en adultos esperando al Sol, luego de la lluvia y sus consecuencias. Porque: "el cielo nos observa/ como a un desnudo abismo, / el agua establece/ su hegemonía celeste".

//

Here are two books by Miguel Avero that the English-speaking reader can immerse themselves in. His initial, consistent, and limpid: *Sawdust Arc*. The domestic, intertextual, and profound: *The Room*. An author, young in age and mature in writing, with seven books to his credit, I am fortunate to know personally and read again, in this hydrating selection by Jona Colson. Here Avero's work is an open window that transforms readers into children looking at the sky and adults waiting for the sun after the rain because: "the sky observes us / like a naked abyss, / water establishes / its celestial hegemony."

–Javier Etchevarren,
Author of *Fable of an Inconsolable Man*

A graceful precision is necessary to transport, intact, the wild magic of Miguel Avero's poetry into English. Jona Colson shows, with his translation of *Aguas/Waters* that he is gloriously up to the task. The poems in this book wash over the reader with the depth and debris of oceans and the pinpoint stinging of tears. "In every man the rain / weaves its argument," they tell us, yet we go on, unable to "know what happens / behind the blinds of others," pieces of a larger puzzle that have come unfastened. Aguas/Waters captures the surreal devastation of living through a time that feels like time ending, with "[w]ater nesting on rooftops" and "settling / around the last fire."

–Francesca Bell, Translation Editor of
The Los Angeles Review and
Marin Country Poet Laureate (CA)

Aguas/Waters flows like the rivers of emotion we sail upon, with Miguel Avero's poems carved into English by Jona Colson to mirror the coastlines and banks crafted by oceans and rivers. Avero's poems sing out memory and heartbreak in these translations, as Colson and Avero remind us that "the old scars/forgotten./We are not the same."

–Serena Agusto-Cox,
Editor of *Mid-Atlantic Review*

Miguel Avero's poems emerge from water. But not cleansing or clarifying waters, rather waters that obscure, erase boundaries, and render the world a vaguely menacing place. "… outside the sky falls without stopping, running down windows the stinging metals / of the rains / its gray curtain." The pages are not forgotten. They fog up. Into this uncertain world, enters Jona Colson, who seems at home here, the details meticulous, umbrellas useless. This is difficult work, without flourish or embroidery, but stoic, exact. Thanks to Jona Colson's keen eye and ear, we are brought face to face with a nightmare, a dark movie.

–Barbara Goldberg, Series Editor,
International Editions, The Word Works

With dream-like, disquieting language, Miguel Avero's poems leave us feeling untethered in a universe where "today every mist rubs us with its lips/ and tomorrow the hurtful/ fangs of the sun/ will tear apart the uselessness of umbrellas." Jona Colson brings the original's stark imagery, rhythms, and subtle humor into a provocative English, as we seamlessly transition between past and present, between exterior and interior landscapes where we come to get a glimpse of the self, imperfect beings that we are.

–Nancy Naomi Carlson, Winner,
2022 Oxford-Weidenfeld Translation Prize

A poet takes great time to write his life in some usable form, to illuminate the diurnal in ways that speak to the eternal, or at the very least provide an evidentiary record of having lived. Avero's delicacy could easily break in a clumsy hand, but Colson's translations uncover, with deep and abiding respect, this stratum of a soul at work, the traceries of Avero's dioramas to time and place and memory.

–Dan Vera, author of *Speaking Wiri Wiri*

COVER DESIGN by Andrew Sargas Klein
BOOK DESIGN and TYPOGRAPHY by Barbara Shaw

ISBN 978-1-941551-39-4

Library of Congress Control Number: 2024932144

Printed in the United States of America

WASHINGTON WRITERS' PUBLISHING HOUSE
2814 5th Street, NE, #1301
Washington, D.C. 20017
More information: www.washingtonwriters.org

DC COMMISSION ON THE ARTS & HUMANITIES

MSAC
DEPARTMENT OF COMMERCE maryland state arts council

PROUD MEMBER

[clmp]
COMMUNITY OF LITERARY MAGAZINES & PRESSES
WWW.CLMP.ORG

Support for Washington Writers' Publishing House comes from the DC Commission on Arts & Humanities, the Maryland State Arts Council, and the Community of Literary Magazines & Presses

ACKNOWLEDGMENTS

My thanks to the magazines and anthologies where many of these poems first appeared, often in earlier versions

América Invertida: A Bilingual Anthology of Younger Uruguayan Poets, University of New Mexico Press, 2017, edited by Jesse Lee Kercheval: "Argumento/Argument," "Aguas/Waters," "Como una Lámina/Like a Sheet," "Ese Mar/That Sea," & "Mar Descascarado/Sea Breaking Open"

Beltway Poetry Quarterly: "Gota a Gota/Drop by Drop"

Chicago Review: "Pluvioteca/Library of Rain" & "Depresión/Depression"

Dispatches: "Hegemonía/Hegemony," "Prólogo/Foreword," "Onírico/Oneiric," & "Ausencias/Absences"

Flyway: Journal of Writing & Environment: "Fermento/Ferment"

International Poetry Review: "Hallazgo/Found"

Los Angeles Review: "Pasillos/Hallways," "Ventanal/Picture Window," "Los que Habitan Este Piso/Those Who Inhabit This Floor," & "Zurita and Dante/ Zurita and Dante"

MAYDAY: "Elección/Choice"

The Mid-Atlantic Review: "Insomne/Insomniac," "La Puerta/The Door," & "Terminal/Terminal"

Palabras Errantes: "Argumento/Argument," "Como una lámina/Like a Sheet," "Los Paraguas/The Umbrellas," "Ese Mar/That Sea," & "Mar Descascarado/Sea Breaking Open"

Plume: "La Pieza/The Room" (published as "La Pieza/The Piece")

Prairie Schooner: "Aguas/Waters"

Tupelo Quarterly: "Testigos/Witnesses," "Arca de aserrín/Sawdust Ark," & "Grises/Grays"

CONTENTS

Part One

ARCA DE ASERRÍN / SAWDUST ARK

Part Two
LA PIEZA/THE ROOM

INTRODUCTION

HOW DID THESE BEAUTIFUL, strange, surreal poems find me? At a recent writer's conference, my workshop instructor, poet Sidney Wade, mentioned that her colleague, Jesse Lee Kercheval, was compiling an anthology of younger Uruguayan poets and was looking for Spanish-English translators. In amazing faith, Sidney passed my name to her, and Jesse Lee read over some of my work, and she invited me to be a part of her project, which became *América Invertida: An Anthology of Emerging Uruguayan Poets*. Jesse Lee paired me with Miguel Avero. I translated his manuscript, *Arca de asserín*, for the anthology, and then, I just kept translating.

This book is a selection from Avero's first two poetry books, *Arca de asserín/Sawdust Ark* and *La Pieza/The Room*. *Aguas/Waters* contains themes similar to these two books: sleeping/wakefulness, dream/reality, dark/light, and past/present. Avero carries on styles and genres of Latin American literature, as well as claiming his own. Many of his poems reflect magical realism, where extraordinary events are accepted as common and not explained. He uses metaphors and similes from the natural world—specifically, a world of water, wet streets, puddles, oceans, storms, thunder, and lightning. This book questions how we exist in the world by inhabiting one space and traveling to another. Many of his poems elevate impressions of the everyday into something beyond what we can only know through language and image.

This collection also highlights a poet at the beginning—his first book for English-speaking readers. With selections from *La Pieza/The Room*, Avero demonstrates maturity in craft and metaphor. He is a prolific contemporary writer in Uruguay—celebrated in his native Montevideo for fiction and hybrid works, as well as poetry. As the smallest Spanish-speaking country in South America, Uruguay is often overshadowed by its bigger, flashier neighbor, Argentina. However, Uruguay, as Uruguayans say themselves, is rich in soccer players and poets.

I live in Washington, D.C., and the area is home to a diverse population with a wide range of linguistic backgrounds. Translation poetry provides a bridge between different cultures and languages, allowing readers to connect with and appreciate the tapestry of global literary traditions. It allows readers to explore the world through poetry and celebrate the region's diversity of voices and languages, and, in this case, the book connects two capitals, D.C. and Montevideo. I'm thrilled to be able to present some of Uruguay's literary wealth to a new English-speaking audience with Washington Writers' Publishing House's first book of translation.

–Jona Colson, Washington, DC

Part One

ARCA DE ASERRÍN / SAWDUST ARK

PRÓLOGO

Extensión de nubarrones en la infancia.
Reducidos a cenizas
los descoloridos días del ayer
absorbidos por tus limpios ojos.
Lo que en aquel tiempo
echó raíces
permanece en un submundo
de impenetrabilidad.

Recapitular sabiendo
que nada vendrá en tu auxilio:
ni los pies de niño aprisionando el pasto
o delineando los costados
desnudos del arroyo,
ni el viento sacudiéndose
como un perro ensopado.

Ya no distingues
el tajo del relámpago en el rostro de la noche.
¿Cómo desenterrar
el cielo sangrante
antes contemplado?

La lluvia prologaba el porvenir
pero éramos niños

sin necesidad de rememorar.

FOREWORD

Extension of thunderclouds in childhood.
Reduced to ashes
the faded days of yesterday
are absorbed by your clear eyes.
What in that time
took root
remains in an underworld
of impenetrability.

Knowing again
that nothing will come to your aid:
neither the feet of a child pressing the grass
or outlining the bare sides
of the stream,
nor the wind shaking
like a drenched dog.

You can no longer distinguish
the slash of lightning in the night's face.
How to dig out
the bleeding sky
contemplated before?

The rain foreshadowed the future
but we were children

with no need to remember.

HEGEMONÍA

Lo que albergó
nuestro corazón
ayer,
fue perdiendo nitidez
en la humedad.

Antes de que el pecho
se convirtiera en piedra,
antes de que en nuestra boca
se acumularan esas ruinas

la misma ventana
apilaba otros momentos.

Detenido en la distancia
todo lo sublime,
aquellos zapatos
errantes
en los que quisiéramos
volver a estar,
las viejas cicatrices
olvidadas.
No somos los mismos.

Paredes que rodearon
infinitos seres
se alojan ahora
amarradas
en nuestro interior,

el cielo nos observa
como a un desnudo abismo,

el agua establece
su hegemonía celeste.

HEGEMONY

What sheltered
our heart
yesterday,
has been losing sharpness
in the humidity.

Before our breast
became stone,
before our mouth
accumulated those ruins

the same window
piled up other moments.

Everything sublime
stopped in the distance,
those shoes
wandering
where we would like
to be again,
the old scars
forgotten.
We are not the same.

Walls that surrounded
infinite beings
are not lodged
moored
inside us,

the sky watches us
like a naked abyss,

the water establishes
its celestial hegemony.

ARGUMENTO

La imagen que echamos
al olvido,
bruma húmeda y ceniza
de cierta tarde envejecida
se agita ahora
ante nosotros.

Todo cuanto pase ante los ojos
llamemos ilusión.
El agua que barre los peldaños,
la prematura noche
oscureciendo el tiempo,
sus manos tintas acosando
las columnas del planeta.

Nunca sabremos lo que ocurre
detrás de las persianas de los otros,
detrás de las pupilas
donde una imagen
remota se desliza
mintiéndonos a todos su verdad.

Las piezas de este puzzle
una a una se desprenden,

sin tregua,

distintas.

En cada hombre la lluvia
teje su argumento.

ARGUMENT

The image that we cast
into oblivion,
wet mist and ash
of a certain aged afternoon,
now stirs
before us.

Everything that passes before our eyes
we call illusion.
The water that sweeps the steps,
the premature night
darkening time,
its ink-stained hands harassing
the columns of the planet.

We will never know what happens
behind the blinds of others,
behind the pupils
where a single image
slides
its truth lying to us all.

The pieces of this puzzle
one by one become detached,

relentlessly

different.

In every man the rain
weaves its argument.

AUSENCIAS

Sus figuras
se esconden sin quererlo.
Aparecen y desaparecen
en el interminable tránsito,
les perdemos la pista,
los volvemos a encontrar.

A simple vista
les quema la vereda gris.

Empapándoles las suelas
el dormido asfalto
es recorrido
por infinitos mares.

Atardece lentamente entre los edificios.

La cegadora luz erige
sombras en el callejón.
En cada construcción,
en cada cubo de piedra levantado,
legiones de seres
buscan subsanar la realidad.

Se tejen mundos ficticios,
entre cicatrices de humedad,
una caja los reúne
como el fogón de antaño

y tarde o temprano
como en un deformado sueño

las reveladas ausencias
desenmascaran soledad.

ABSENCES

Their figures
hide unwillingly.
They appear and disappear
in the interminable traffic,
we lose sight of them,
we find them again.

To the naked eye
they are burned by the gray sidewalk.

Soaking our soles
the sleeping asphalt
is the route
of infinite seas.

Slowly the sun sets between buildings.

The blinding light sets up
shadows in the alley.
With each construction,
with each block of stone raised,
legions of beings
seek to heal reality.

They weave fictional worlds,
among humidity's scars,
a box gathers them together
like the fire of long ago

and sooner or later
as in a deformed dream

the absences revealed
unmask loneliness.

AGUAS

Agua en la mañana alquitranada

o en la noche que cubre
de cartones el amanecer.

Agua en los tejados anidando.

Agua en la explanada
donde olvidaron sus agujeros
negros las estrellas.

Agua incesante,
agua de a ratos.

Agua en el reflejo
que descubre
el ojo en el espejo.

Agua en la tinta de los versos
que no se escribirán nunca.

Agua rebasando
el vaso frío y ahogado
con una gota inestimable.

Agua en el revuelto río
de nuestra paz interior,
donde jamás caminaremos,
donde ni cenizas quedan.

Agua acampando
en torno al último fogón.

WATERS

Water in the tar-dark morning

or the night that covers the sunrise
with boxes.

Water nesting on rooftops.

Water in the plaza
where the stars
forgot their black holes.

Constant water,
occasional water.

Water in the reflection
that discovers
the eye in the mirror.

Water in the ink of the verses
that will never be written.

Water overflowing
the cold glass and drowned
with an immensurable drop.

Water in the troubled river
of our inner peace,
where we will never walk,
where no ashes remain.

Water settling
around the last fire.

GRISES

Es gris la madrugada
y este amor
y este dolor
y este recuerdo
es gris.

Sentir la soledad
caer desde esa bóveda
blindada gota a gota.
La lluvia errante
y ahora la lluvia es gris.

¿Pero para qué tanto pasado?
¿Por qué recordar parado en un día así?

Mientras afuera
se descascara
el cielo sin cesar,

se corren las ventanas,
los punzantes
metales de la lluvia,
su acero líquido,
su cortina gris.

Gris es la envoltura del olvido
y todo lo perdido es gris.

GRAYS

Dawn is gray
and this love
and this pain
and this memory
is gray.

Feel the loneliness
fall from that armored
vault drop by drop.
The wandering rain
and now the rain is gray.

But why so much past?
Why remember standing on such a day?

While outside
the sky falls
without stopping,

running down the windows,
the piercing
metals of the rain,
its liquid steel,
its gray curtain.

Gray is the wrapping of oblivion
and all that is lost is gray.

MAR DESCASCARADO

Se desintegra la noche
sobre el resplandor de los paraguas,
sobre las innumerables pieles
poco a poco endurecidas.
En los pliegues de la estremecida brisa
aire y agua son lo mismo.
Individuos apurados
pisoteando los espejos
perplejos de la calle.
Nocturna luz
que un humo gris ha suplantado.
La mueca del hombre
en cada esquina
reunida
ante un cielo
desmoronado tantas veces.
El niño y su sonrisa
tras una ventana azul
como el sueño de los peces
y encima de la tierra
un mar descascarado.

SEA BREAKING OPEN

The night disintegrates
over the brightness of the umbrellas,
over the countless skins
gradually hardened.
In the folds of the quivering breeze
air and water are the same.
Rushed individuals
trampling the perplexed
mirrors of the street.
Nocturnal light
that the gray smoke has replaced.
A man's grimace
at each corner
gathered
under a sky
collapsed so many times.
The child and his smile
behind a blue window
like the dream of fish
and above the earth
a sea breaking open.

ONÍRICO

Ni tu regreso a la tierra casi invisible,
ni el camino sin retorno de tus dedos
en el azul de los cristales,
pudieron volver sombrías
las paredes de mis sueños.

Ni las indefensas nubes
mecidas por el viento,

ni el cuaderno mojado
con mis desteñidos garabatos.

Tampoco aquellos ojos
simulando
tus líquidas esferas

o el perro merodeando
las esquinas
despiadadas del invierno.

Pero un día
la cosecha negra
crecerá en mi predio,

guardaré en mi armario
el arma fría

y reconoceré en mis gestos
los indicios de esta tarde

que tras las fisuras
de un recuerdo
habrá dejado de ser mía.

ONEIRIC

Neither your return to the almost invisible earth,
nor the fleeting path of your fingers
in the blue of the crystals,
could turn the walls
of my dreams somber.

Nor the helpless
wind-blown clouds,

Nor the wet notebook
with my faded drawings.

Not those eyes
simulating
your watery spheres

or the dog prowling
the ruthless corners
of winter.

But one day
the black harvest
will grow on my land,

I'll put the cold gun away
in my closet

and I will recognize in my gestures
the signs of this afternoon

that after the fissures
of a memory
will no longer be mine.

TESTIGOS

Mirar y sin pensarlo
entornar los ojos
ante un sinfín
de caricias derramadas.

El pan se fue desmigajando.

Hay bocas y no las hay
donde la mano
inconcebible lo reparte.
Yo estoy ahí,

puedo masticar la sal y sonreír
ante un ventanal hecho añicos,
frente a los vertidos
fragmentos
quebrados en la hierba.

Trepan los ojos
un ensamblaje interminable
sin resquicios de claridad.
Nos alcanza a todos
el mismo lodo.

Somos testigos
mudos de esta prisa,

como si no fueran
astillas
clavándose en la piel,
como si no fueran
estacas
hundiéndose en la tierra.

WITNESSES

Look and without thinking
your eyes squint
before endless
spilled caresses.

The bread started crumbling.

There are mouths and there are none
where the inconceivable hand
distributes it.
I'm there,

I can chew the salt and smile
in front of a shattered window,
in front of the spilled
fragments
broken in the grass.

Eyes climb
an endless assembly
with no chasms of clarity.
The same mud
reaches us all.

We are witnesses
speechless from this haste

as if they were not
splinters
nailing into the skin,
as if they were not
stakes
plunging into the earth.

ARCA DE ASERRÍN

Te descubrirán mil veces
tras excavar en la memoria.

Sea de quien sea
será tuyo
el dormido costillar,
el esqueleto esparcido
entre los montes milenarios.

Es el ayer
el espacio mítico de tu existencia.
La orfandad de presente y porvenir.

Aunque en ti se posó
la madre de todas las lluvias
y entre todos los rostros viste
las más oscuras
máscaras del cielo,

bajo un abanico de tormentas,
sea de quien sea
será tuyo
el cuerpo a medio sepultar.

Las fauces azules
no pudieron devorarte nunca
por más que la lluvia crepitaba
como un incendio interminable.

Alboroto y miedo
en el corazón de los casales,
los maderos castigados
por pezuñas y musgo,
todo es en la arena
leyenda y aserrín.

SAWDUST ARK

They will discover you a thousand times
after digging in the memory.

Whoever you are
it will be yours
the sleeping rib,
the skeleton scattered
among the ancient mountains.

It is yesterday
the mythical space of your existence.
Orphan of present and future.

Although in you settled
the mother of all the rains,
and between all the faces you saw
the darkest
masks of the sky,

under a range of storms,
whoever it may belong to,
it will be yours
the half-buried body.

The blue jaws
could never devour you
even if than the rain crackled
like an endless fire.

Noise and fear
in the heart of the houses,
the timbers punished
by hooves and moss,
everything is in the sand
legend and sawdust.

COMO UNA LÁMINA

se retiró el océano,
todo resurgió con su rostro más violento,
con su cara de nada,
con su quietud de muerte.

Vidas que se volvieron piedra
de amar las profundidades,
misterio develado,
cristal de falsa diafanidad.

Montañas que se hicieron pequeñas,
casas que lucieron peces en sus ventanas
y desde ahora la imposibilidad

de valorar una moneda,
de señalar el arcoíris,
o de confiar en pactos.

LIKE A SHEET

the ocean withdrew,
all resurfaced with its most violent face,
with its face of nothing,
with its stillness of death.

Lives that turned to stone
from love of the depths,
mystery unveiled,
crystal of false clarity.

Mountains that became small,
houses that show fish in the windows,
and from now the impossibility

of valuing a coin,
of pointing at the rainbow,
or of trusting agreements.

LOS PARAGUAS

Ciudad de cielo en sombras,
tapizada inútilmente por manos
que de pronto se muestran arrugadas.

Tanto líquido tacto sobre los cuerpos,
desde abajo los paraguas
enseñan sus espaldas.

Viejos perros que ladraron
a desaparecidas lunas
debajo de un ciprés.

Fue guarida, fue testigo,
fue encubridor,
su misión fue siempre ir escondiendo
pero ha muerto,
y tumbado apenas puede
ocultar su propia sombra.

Ahora todos haremos leña de él.

Aunque mañana se sucedan

una a una las tormentas,

sólo los paraguas permanecerán de pie.

THE UMBRELLAS

City of sky in shadows,
uselessly covered by hands
that suddenly are wrinkled.

So much liquid touch over the bodies,
they show their backs
from under the umbrellas.

Old dogs that barked
at disappearing moons
under a cypress.

It was a hideout, it was a witness,
it was a cover,
its mission was always to go on hiding
but it has died,
and fallen can only
cover its own shadow.

Now we will make firewood from it.

Although tomorrow, when the storms come

one by one,

only the umbrellas will remain standing.

INSOMNE

Azules sueños cruzan la habitación a oscuras
formando el rostro de las noches
en un cielo de humedad.

Alimenta el viento
la voz del aguacero,
surca mis oídos y enardece
la tenacidad de mis ideas.

Pretendo buscar
un cegador momento
o punto ciego
en que no acosen más estas paredes,
en que no apunten más estas ventanas,

como si fuera posible
guarecerse de esa sombra

y nunca te enteraras
cuánto me acompañas.

INSOMNIAC

Blue dreams cross the room in the dark
forming the face of the nights
in a humid sky.

The voice of the downpour
feeds the wind,
it rides through my ears and inflames
the tenacity of my ideas.

I intend to search for
a blinding moment
or a blind spot
where these walls no longer harass,
where these windows no longer point,

as if it were possible
to shelter from that shadow

and you'd never find out
how much you accompany me.

ESE MAR

Ese mar profundo entre nosotros
o distancia que nos une
sin remedio,

aire quieto y bajo
como una calle donde cruzaron las palabras.
Esquina que algún día tendremos que enfrentar;

rendir cuentas de los últimos abrazos
cuando estos se hayan extinguido,

las últimas cenizas grises de los besos,
los últimos sonidos
de un fino llover que era
capa y felicidad.

Por más
que a aquel tiempo le llamamos intemperie
y a la suave brisa aquella
le decíamos silencio.

THAT SEA

That deep sea between us
or distance that unites us
without hope,

still and low air
like a street where the words crossed.
A corner we will someday have to face

to account for the last embraces
when they are extinguished,

the last gray ashes of the kisses,
the last sounds
of a fine rain that was
a coat and happiness.

Even though
we called that bad weather
and the gentle breeze
we named silence.

GOTA A GOTA

Tierra nublada de pasos.
Inercia de mi andar,
seguridad de huellas que no veo.

No miro hacia atrás, no giro mi cabeza,
sólo siento en el rostro
un finísimo tejido de agua y aire,

es allí donde me dejo caer,
donde el viento se siente
golpeado por mi cuerpo,

más allá de los abrazos
imperceptibles de los árboles,
tan cerca de la doble caricia
del lomo de mi perro,

reteniendo silencios y destilaciones,
emanaciones últimas y sombras
de un día que se agota

gota
a
gota
tan feliz.

DROP BY DROP

Land clouded by steps.
Inertia of my walk,
safety of footprints I do not see.

I don't look back, I don't turn my head,
on my face I only feel
the fine fabric of water and air,

it is there where I let myself fall
where the wind feels
beaten by my body,

beyond the imperceptible
embraces of the trees,
so close to the double caress
of my dog's back,

holding silences and distillations,
final emanations and shadows
of a day that washes away

drop
by
drop
so happy.

ELECCIÓN

Renunciar a ello o salir a confrontar:
calma o tempestad,
ocaso o alba.

Salir sin saber que salía ni a qué;
y quién sabe qué fue lo que dejé
con mi partida.

Porque hoy cada bruma nos roza con sus labios
y mañana los hirientes
colmillos del sol
desgarrarán la inutilidad de los paraguas.

Abandonados,
sobre este día abandonados.
Con pies para agrietar la carretera,
con palabras para derramar en un cuaderno,
con pecados para enterrar bajo los árboles.

CHOICE

Give it up or go out and confront it:
calm or storm,
sunset or dawn.

Go out without knowing I was going out or why;
and who knows what I left
with my departure.

Because today every mist rubs us with its lips
and tomorrow the hurtful
fangs of the sun
will tear apart the uselessness of umbrellas.

Abandoned,
on this day abandoned.
With feet to crack the road,
with words to spill in a notebook,
with sins to bury under the trees.

Part Two

LA PIEZA/THE ROOM

LA PIEZA

Hace algunos años
pinté de gris la habitación.

Tallé las gotas
con el martillo de Dufresne.

Hoy todos los desagües mueren
en la ventana sur,
veo el casamiento de los zorros,
y el cielo de Teillier.

Pero también
algunas veces,
en sonámbulos descuidos

pude ver el sol;

hoy lo tapo con un dedo.

THE ROOM

Some years ago
I painted the room gray.

I carved the drops
with the hammer of Dufresne.

Today all the drains die
in the south window,
I see the wedding of the foxes,
and the sky of Teillier.

But also
sometimes,
in sleepwalking carelessness

I could see the sun;

today I cover it with a finger.

LA PUERTA

"Los de dentro non les querien tornar palabra"
— Cantar del Cid

Despego mis persianas
desde el colchón
de antiguas fornicaciones,

el pestillo manoseado
por las manos idas.

No hay noche anterior.

Eco de mi voz llamando,
eco del silencio respondiendo,
pero ninguna niña
se acercara con instrucciones.

Observar acurrucado...
(toda sonrisa es un umbral)
desterrándome a mí mismo.

Atrás,
muy atrás quedan
miedos y demonios

y mis peores fotografías
en el placar.

THE DOOR

"Those inside do not want to make a word"
      – Cantar del Cid

I take off my blinds
from the mattress
of ancient fornications,

the groped doorknob
by the vanished hands.

There is no previous night.

Echo of my voice calling,
echo of silence responding,
but no girl
approached with instructions.

Observe curled up ...
(every smile is a threshold)
banishing myself.

Behind,
left far behind
fears and demons

and my worst pictures
in the closet.

PASILLOS

Iré por los pasillos
haciendo caso omiso
de los charcos transparentes,
de las eléctricas guiñadas,
de los derruidos calefactores.

Cada puerta esconde un mundo
pero no puedo elegir,
apenas un puntapié en alguna de ellas,
antes de regresar corriendo
y tropezar,
chocar, insultar

al dios que sale
de los ascensores
con la bolsa de pan
y la botella de vino.

Mi habitación no tiene
descripción ni número,
solo un flujo que se escapa
por debajo de la puerta.

HALLWAYS

I will go through the corridors
paying no attention
to the transparent puddles,
the electric winks,
the destroyed heaters.

Each door hides a world,
but I cannot choose,
I just kick some of them,
before running back
and stumbling,
crashing, insulting

the god that comes out
of the elevators
with the bag of bread
and the bottle of wine.

My room does not have
a description or a number,
only a current that escapes
below the door.

10 F

Si viviera en el 10 F,
habitación en sepia,
con espejos de agua sucia
y cerraduras rotas

y me encontrara con jota Connelly
caminando entre los charcos
de su propio sueño,

y de su rostro se descolgara la lluvia
y del mío la fascinación,

pensaría que yo también
soy pieza de algún sueño

o pesadilla

o película oscura

con paredes tatuadas de humedad
y un espeso y ahogado
cántico de niña en *Aguas turbias*.

10 F

If I lived in 10 F,
the room in sepia,
with dirty water mirrors
and broken locks

and I met J. Connolly
walking among the puddles
of her own dream,

and from her face the rain came down
and from mine the fascination,

I would think that I too
am a part of some dream

or nightmare

or dark movie

with walls tattooed with moisture
and a thick and drowned
girl's song in *Dark Water*.

RANGO DE EXISTENCIA

Nombrar los olvidados y no vistos cimientos.
Frente a los espejos Candyman.

Nombrar paredes, bloques que se elevan.
Barro, golpes, taquicardia.

Nombrar puerta, pestillo y cerradura.
Desnuda, sexo, cenizas, sábanas.

Nombrar un techo empequeñeciendo noches.
Centinelas, cuervos, ilusiones, máscaras.

RANGE OF EXISTENCE

Name the forgotten and unseen foundations.
In front of the Candyman mirrors.

Name walls, blocks that rise.
Mud, blows, tachycardia.

Name door, doorknob and lock.
Naked, sex, ashes, sheets.

Name a roof diminishing nights.
Sentinels, crows, illusions, masks.

VENTANAL

La soledad de este sitio,
el abuso de silencios...

He visto algunos habitantes
errando por los pasillos,
he llegado a la conclusión
de que les temo.

Siempre tranco la puerta de mi pieza,
las madrugadas se hacen largas
entre arañas que deambulan
por el cielo raso.

Una noche por el ala norte,
un ventanal abría
dos inmensos párpados rojos,

ascendí por la rampa oscura,

vi mi propia sombra
tirada como estiércol en la calle,
un gajo de luna delator,

suspiré,
hablé,

todo giraba en torno a mi persona.

PICTURE WINDOW

The loneliness of this place,
the abuse of silences ...

I have seen some people
wandering through the corridors,
I have come to the conclusion
that I fear them.

I always lock the door of my room,
dawns are long
among spiders that roam
through the ceiling.

One night in the north wing,
a picture window opened
two huge red eyelids,

I climbed up the dark ramp,

I saw my own shadow
thrown like dung in the street,
a telltale slice of the moon,

I sighed,
I talked,

everything revolved around me.

ESCALERAS

Las escaleras
se estremecen
parkinsonianamente,

dispuestas de manera irrepetible;

siempre hay peldaños flojos
que conducen al temor,
a la noche,
al desacierto
de seres imperfectos.

STAIRS

The stairs'
parkinsonian
shudder

arranged repeatedly;

there are always loose steps
that lead to fear,
to the night,
to the mistake
of imperfect beings.

302

Mi amigo Henry Townshend
con el cabello desaliñado,

con el vaquero sucio
y la camisa desprolija.

Caminaría por pasillos
color lava pateando perros
asesinos,

espiaría a Eileen mientras
cabalga sobre un conejo rosa,

y no llamaría a un sanitario
por el boquete en su bañera.

Mi amigo Henry,
en plena madrugada,

dejaría pendiente
una cópula insigne,
o una novela barata,

y saldría a fotografiar iglesias
entre el humo de Centralia.

302

My friend Henry Townshend
with disheveled hair,

with the dirty jeans
and the untidy shirt.

He would walk through blood-
stained corridors
kicking dogs,

he would spy on Eileen while
she rode on a pink rabbit,

and would not call a plumber
for the hole in her bathtub.

My friend Henry,
in the middle of the night,

would leave before
a notable copulation,
or a cheap novel,

and would go out to photograph churches
amid the smoke of Centralia.

PLUVIOTECA

Nada Thiago Rocca en el primer estante
junto a Laura y su *Llamar*
al agua por su nombre.

La *Biblia* diluvia universal.

Llueve en un verso de Pizarnik,
en un fragmento de Cortázar,
en un poema de Peri Rossi.

No hay polvo sino gotas,
y musgo
y cañadas intertextuales.

Las páginas no se olvidan,

se empañan.

LIBRARY OF RAIN

Nothing Thiago Rocca on the first shelf
with Laura and her *Calling
Water By Its Name.*

The Bible floods universally.

It rains in a verse from Pizarnik,
in an excerpt of Cortázar,
in a poem by Peri Rossi.

There is no dust but drops,
and moss
and intertextual ravines.

The pages are not forgotten,

they fog up.

DEPRESIÓN

Advertir la cercanía de un pestillo,
seguir el golpe de luz que se propaga
como una larga melena de fuego,
como una insinuación de la salida.

Indagar el otro lado,
el barniz de la puerta de enfrente
con la frontal silueta de nuestra sombra.

Carezco de la llave y el ave
y el sol de mayo
en el hemisferio norte;

depresiones ballesteras,

aquí los dioses no suelen
ir asignando galardones.

DEPRESSION

Notice the closeness of a doorknob,
follow the light stroke that spreads
like a long mane of fire,
like the hint of an exit.

Inquire on the other side,
the varnish on the front door
with our front-facing silhouette.

I lack the key and the bird
and the sun of May
in the northern hemisphere;

crossbow depressions,

here the gods don't usually
assign awards.

LOS QUE HABITAN ESTE PISO

Tienen el privilegio de beber
con Chinasky las cervezas
azules de Teillier.

Marcos vacíos
de sus habitaciones,
floreros destrozados
en las mesitas de luz;

nieblas de nicotina,
poesía,
y los gusanos
adentro de las botellas.

Los que habitan este piso
deben dormir
tras recitar
nevados poemas de Celan

en alemán.

THOSE WHO INHABIT THIS FLOOR

They have the privilege of drinking
Teillier's blue beers
with Chinasky.

Empty frames
of their rooms,
shattered vases
on the bedside tables;

nicotine mists,
poetry,
and the worms
inside the bottles

Those who inhabit this floor
must sleep
after reciting
snowy poems by Celan

in German.

ZURITA AND DANTE

"...pero pasó que estaba en un baño cuando vi algo como un ángel ..."
– Raúl Zurita, *Purgatorio*

Asciende hacia la luz Zurita andante
pule los escalones Zurita andante
hiede a hipoclorito Zurita andante
pantalón con lamparones Zurita andante.

Divisa el color rojo Zurita andante
lucha con la manchas Zurita andante
y el aliento de los caños Zurita andante.

Escribe un poema Zurita andante
canta a los azulejos Zurita andante.

En el baño de mujeres Zurita andante
engrameando la tiesta Zurita andante
descubre las virtudes Zurita andante

ya no tendrá sueños Zurita andante.

ZURITA AND DANTE

"... but it happened that I was in a bathroom when I saw something like an angel ..."   – Raúl Zurita, *Purgatory*

Ascending toward the light Zurita walks
polishing the steps Zurita walks
stinking of Clorox Zurita walks
with stained pants Zurita walks.

Seeing red Zurita walks
fighting with stains Zurita walks
and smelling like drains Zurita walks.

Writing a poem Zurita walks
singing to the tiles Zurita walks.

In the women's bathroom Zurita walks
shaking his head Zurita walks
discovering virtue Zurita walks

No longer dreaming Zurita walks.

HALLAZGO

Encontré a un hombre que recitaba un poema

de un poemario inconcluso,
su mejor poema;

y vi que mientras lo recitaba
lo componía
y sus palabras se escribían en mi cerebro
y salían de mi boca
y de todos mis gestos

y mi voz resonaba en ese pequeño mundo solitario
donde yacía sólo mi propio cuerpo,
mi sola mente y mi poema

que hablaba sobre un hombre que encontraba a otro,
que era él mismo
recitando
de su inconcluso poemario
su mejor poema.

FOUND

I found a man who recited a poem

from an unfinished book of poems,
his best poem;

and I saw that while he recited it
he composed it
and his words were written in my brain
and they came out of my mouth
and of all my gestures

and my voice echoed in that little lonely world
where only my own body lay,
my lone mind and my poem

that talked about a man who found another,
that was himself
reciting
from his unfinished book of poems
his best poem.

MUJERES DE HELMUT

"Las mujeres no suelen vivir ante una sábana blanca."
– Helmut Newton

Incontables cuerpos
de mujeres me rodean,
desnudos totales
o con alguna minúscula prenda.

Los espejos reflejan la perfección,
sacralizan lo físico;
yo había desaparecido en la pieza,
apenas un rastro de mis pisadas
entre las mujeres de Helmut,

mujeres en blanco y negro
enseñando sus pechos
entre pitadas de cigarrillos,
mujeres de fina
y escurridiza lencería,

las mujeres de Helmut Newton,
siempre
con los tacos altos elevándose
y elevándose

queriendo acaparar en ellas
el flash de la belleza.

THE WOMEN OF HELMUT

"Women do not usually live before a white sheet."
   – Helmut Newton

Countless bodies
of women surround me,
total nudes
or with some tiny garment.

Mirrors reflect perfection,
they sacralize the physical;
I had disappeared in the room,
just a trace of my footsteps
among the women of Helmut,

women in black and white
showing their breasts
between cigarette puffs,
women with fine
and slippery lingerie,

the women of Helmut Newton,
always
with high heels rising
and rising

wanting to keep for themselves
the flash of beauty.

FERMENTO

Y es verdad que ella se cansa,
sus oídos padecen ese tan mío retroceder,
se angustia tras percibir
un tropel de pensamientos, lejos,
más allá de las barcas de estos nuevos años,

cuando no había ni farmacias ni calles picadas por el frío,

(y el coro de los perros
al unísono)

cuando no existía un atalaya de madera oculto entre los pinos
y los sauces,

(y el canto de los gallos
al unísono)

y el silencio del que piensa
al unísono.

FERMENT

And it's true that she gets tired,
and what her ears suffer is his recoiling,
she is distressed after perceiving
a crowd of thoughts, far away,
beyond the boats of these new years,

when there were no pharmacies or streets scarred by the cold,

(and the chorus of the dogs
in unison)

when there was no wooden watchtower hidden among the pines
and the willows,

(and the crowing of the roosters
in unison)

and from the silence she thinks
in unison.

AGITACIÓN

Ay de este magnánimo insomne,
de este huidizo loco que recorre
las habitaciones,

rasga las cortinas y corroe
las despensas
sin descanso,

como las arañas y los espejos,
como los relojes, canas y rajaduras
sin descanso,

como la creciente levadura del deterioro,
sin descanso.

AGITATION

Woe to this magnanimous insomniac,
this elusive madman who walks
the rooms,

tears the curtains and corrodes
the pantry
without rest,

like spiders and mirrors,
like the watches, gray hair, and cracks
without a rest,

like the rising yeast of decay,
without rest.

TERMINAL

Al oeste de las escaleras, donde yace la tumba marítima
o un libro que no se termina de albergar nunca,
veremos la alfombra pisada por el lautarino,
por el raptor de una chica que debió llamarse Dolores;
españoles de una España, ahora, carabelas blancas, que
coparon la mansión deshabitada entrando por la noche
a través de las ventanas mal cerradas,
manchadas heridas escarbadas, vidrios que sudan sangrantes,
paredes peladas por dentro, por fuera arropadas
como el cuerpo tiritante de un sonámbulo, de un loco que resiste
por los temblores de la casa, latido incesante de las lámparas
corazón erguido y hervido como un sexo,
mampara de sol infatigable tras las cortinas,
rojas cortinas de fuego inconmensurable, terco, creador y frío fuego,
fuego para apagar el agua, agua para prender el fuego,
iluminación instantánea de un paraíso, de un rojo prado
sin locus amoenus, sin infierno prometido, ni del héroe los mitemas,
con tuberías donde circula la sangre enrojeciendo los sitios por donde pasa,
dejando cada pieza en cuarentena y empantanando
el virus en las escalinatas
como un azote de infierno a invierno
como una azotea imposible por la noche coronada.

TERMINAL

West of the stairs, where the maritime tomb lies
or a book that is never finished,
we will see the carpet stepped on by the lautarino,
by the kidnapper of a girl who must have been named Dolores;
Spaniards of a Spain, now, white caravels, that
took over the uninhabited mansion at night
through the poorly closed windows,
stained scraped wounds, glass that sweats blood,
walls bare inside, covered outside
like the shivering body of a sleepwalker, of a madman who resists
the tremors of the house, the incessant beat of the lamps
heart erect and boiled like sex,
a tireless sun that goes through the curtains,
red curtains of immeasurable fire, stubborn, creative and cold fire,
fire to put out the water, water to light the fire,
instantaneous illumination of a paradise, of a red meadow
without locus, without the promised hell, nor the hero's myths,
with pipes where blood circulates reddening the places where it passes,
leaving each room in quarantine and bogging down
the virus on the steps
like a whip from hell to winter
like an impossible rooftop crowned by the night.

AGRADECIMIENTOS/THANKS

Miguel Avero

Aguas es el coherente título para unos textos que se han abierto paso por recovecos impensados, ajenos al chaparrón antiguo que los concibió. Quiero agradecer a Jona Colson por su esfuerzo y dedicación, y por su poesía que se ha entremezclado con la mía en sus bellísimas traducciones. Agradecer también a la línea que me condujo a él: Laura Cesarco Eglin y Jesse Lee Kercheval. Por último, mi gratitud para the Washington Writers' Publishing House, mar afectuoso donde navegan mis palabras.

//

Jona Colson

Thank you to the Washington Writers' Publishing House for supporting this first work of translation for the press and for myself as a translator. Specifically, thank you to Caroline Bock and Kathleen Wheaton for believing in this project, and for the edits and time.

Also, huge thanks to the poets and professors who introduced me to Miguel Avero and supported and mentored me, Sidney Wade and Jesse Lee Kercheval. And more huge thanks to poet/professor Laura Cesarco Eglin for the fine edits, time, and advice.

Also, to the teachers and professors that inspired my love of Spanish and literature: Rebecca Stoner, Carol Leach, Deborah Azizi, Cristina Sáenz de Tejada, Judy Collier, and Myra Sklarew. You have all made me love language and reading and writing.

Also, to all the journals and editors who published and encouraged these poems. I thank you for your work and time.

Great thanks to those who have supported WWPH in 2024 and helped make this publication possible: James Kronzer, Thomas Qualey, Jack Curry, Bob & Janice Fries, Jim & Connie Qualey, Grace Cavalieri, and Sandra Beasley.

And, of course, to Miguel Avero, for his words, craft, and imagination.

Miguel Avero, was born in Montevideo, Uruguay in 1984, and is a poet, narrator, essayist, teacher, and researcher. He is the co-founder of Orientación Poesía and On the Path of Dogs. He directs the writing workshop, "Puerta Quimera," and has appeared in various national and international anthologies. He has published various collections of poems, including *Arca de aserrín* (Ediciones en blanco; 2011; republished in 2021 by Ediciones del Demiurgo), and the novella, *Michaela Moon* (Travesia Ediciones, 2014; republished in 2015). In 2016, Avero published the books *Let Nobody Ask About You* (Bestial Barracuda Babilonica, poetic prose) and *La Pieza* (Walkie Talkie Ediciones, poetry). He won the first Espacio Mixtura poetry prize with the book *Libreta insomne* (Editorial Primero de Mayo, 2019). In 2020, he published *Haiku mate* (Ediciones del Demiurgo, poetry) co-authored with the Minuan Poet, Leonardo de Leon. In 2022, *Prosperidad*, a hybrid text of poetry, essays, and memoirs, was released by Ginko Ediroia. Recently, by the same publishing house, the book of short stories *Michaela Moon y otros tentativas* (2023) was published. Much of Avero's work has been translated into English and French.

Jona Colson is an educator and poet. His poetry collection, *Said Through Glass*, won the Jean Feldman poetry prize from the Washington Writers' Publishing House. His poems, translations, and interviews have appeared in *The Southern Review*, *Ploughshares*, *LitHub*, and elsewhere. He is currently a professor at Montgomery College in Maryland where he teaches English as a Second Language. He is co-president of the Washington Wrtiers' Publishing House and poetry editor of *WWPH Writes*. He lives in Washington, DC.

Washington Writers' Publishing House is a non-profit, cooperative literary organization that has published over 100 volumes of poetry since 1975 as well as fiction and nonfiction. The press sponsors three annual competitions for writers living in DC, Maryland, and Virginia, and the winners of each category (one each in poetry, fiction, and creative nonfiction) comprise our annual slate. In 2021, WWPH launched an online literary journal, WWPH WRITES to expand our mission to further the creative work of writers in our region. In 2024, WWPH launched our biennial works in translation series. More about the Washington Writers' Publishing House at www.washingtonwriters.org

www.ingramcontent.com/pod-product-compliance
Lightning Source LLC
Chambersburg PA
CBHW022015080426
42733CB00007B/610